US Immigration Exam Study Guide in English and French

Michael Swedenberg

Copyright © 2023 James Michael Swedenberg
All rights reserved.

Contact me at: Mike@Swedenberg.com

Twitter: @USAcitizenship

US Immigration Exam Study Guide in English and French

100 Questions and Answers to the US Immigration Test in English and French

A unique product, professionally developed and annotated.

Lists all current Senators, Governors and State Capitols plus Legal Advice

Michael Swedenberg

Study Guide
100 Questions and Answers for the US Immigration Test in English and French
A unique product, professionally developed and annotated

The U.S. Citizenship Services (USCIS) administers a verbal test to all immigrants applying for citizenship. This study guide tutors French speaking immigrants for the USCIS verbal citizenship test in English and French. The questions have been selected from questions used on past exams by the USCIS.

Les 100 questions civiques (histoire et gouvernement) et les réponses pour l'examen nouvellement désigné sont listées à continuation. Les candidats qui ont rempli la Forme pour Naturalisation, Forme N-400, le 1er Octobre ou après doivent étudier cette liste. L'examen civique est un examen oral et l'officier du USCIS (Services de Citoyenneté et d'Immigration des Etats-Unis D'Amérique) demandera 10 questions des 100 questions civiques. Un candidat devra répondre à 6 questions des 10 questions correctement pour passer la portion civique de l'examen de citoyenneté.

Même si USCIS sait qu'il peut y avoir plusieures réponses correctes au 100 questions civiques, les candidats sont encouragés á repondre aux questions civiques en utilisant les réponses suivantes.

Studying these questions does not guarantee obtaining citizenship to the United States.

Bi Lingual Languages available:
Spanish, English only, Polish, Albanian, French, Portuguese, Russian, Korean, Chinese, Vietnamese and Tagalog.

DEDICATION

Dedicated to all those wishing to become American Citizens

CONTENTS

INTRODUCTION 1

Advice 2

AMERICAN GOVERNMENT 17

GOUVERNEMENT AMERICAIN 17

System of Government 20

    Le Système de Gouvernement 20

AMERICAN HISTORY 32

    HISTOIRE AMÉRICAINE 32

INTEGRATED CIVICS 40

    ETUDES CIVIQUES INTEGREES 40

    Geography / Geographie 40

    Symbols / Signes 42

    Holidays. / Jours fériés 42

SAMPLE WRITTEN SENTENCES 43

Members of the Senate 45

    Senators of the 118th Congress 47

List of State Governors 52

List of State Capitols 55

ABOUT THE AUTHOR 58

ACKNOWLEDGMENTS

We are grateful for the cooperation of the

U.S. Citizenship Services (USCIS)

.

INTRODUCTION

The 100 sample questions and answers for the US Immigration test are listed below. The test is an oral exam in which the USCIS Officer will ask you up to 10 of the 100 questions. You must answer six out of ten questions correctly to pass the civics portion of the test.

On the naturalization test, some answers may change because of elections or appointments. As you study for the test, make sure that you know the most current members of Congress, Senate, Speaker of the House and Governor of your state and district.

This publication is the only study guide that provides this information and updates it throughout the year.

We also provide you with the Sample Written Questions which all applicants must know how to write in English.

Advice

from the Immigration Law offices of

KURCZABA LAW OFFICES P.C.

6219 N. Milwaukee - Chicago, IL 60646

10661 S. Roberts Rd., Palos Hills, IL 60465

(773) 774-0000

www.kurczabalaw.com

BECOMING A CITIZEN

The day of your interview, you will be asked to appear at a

specific date and time at the

Immigration Office. For interviews in Chicago, our interview

will take place at:

101 W. Ida B. Wells (formerly Congress Parkway), 3rd Floor

Chicago

Bring to the interview:

Interview notice

Passports – all your passports, current and expired

Permanent Resident Card (green card)

Driver's License/ ID

Income Tax Returns – bring your last 5 years of tax returns (may be asked)

Alimony/Child Support – (if required to pay) – bring proof of payment Check In:

Arrive 30 minutes before your scheduled interview

Check in with the receptionist (in Chicago - on the 3rd floor) – they will give you a number

You will be called by number

Interview:

When called, you will enter the officer's room, and:

Oath – swear that you will tell the truth.

Fingerprint /identification– the officer will take your photograph (using a digital camera) and ask you to place your left and right index finger on a little black box on their desk.

Administer the following test

1.TEST

Questions – 100 possible Questions – as listed in this book

You will be given 10 questions - 2 from each section,

You must have 6 correct. As soon as you have 6 correct – you pass and the question portion of the test ends.

Reading- you will be asked to read a question out loud to the officer (usually shown on an iPad)

Writing – you will be asked to write a sentence on the same iPad which is dictated to you. (in Chicago – this is often the answer to the question you just read)

2.APPLICATION

You will be asked questions from the Citizenship Application (form N400).

Biographical information

Name (your full name – first, middle last) as shown on your birth certificate

Any other names used – including your maiden (before marriage) name

Address, telephone,

Your marital status

Spouse's name, date of birth, date of marriage, immigration status (if out of status – you may state this, you may also state that you are applying for permanent residency for them). If your spouse is a US Citizen already, you may bring a copy of their Naturalization Certificate

Children – their names, dates of birth, locations of birth, current address (often city is sufficient)

Details on employment, residency

Travel History – when is the last time you left the United States? Sometimes officers will ask you have you left the United States since filing your N-400 application? OR Have you ever been outside of the United States for 180 days or longer? You may check your travel history on the Customs and Border Protection Website at:

https://i94.cbp.dhs.gov/I94/#/home

If you have been outside of the United States for longer than 180 days at any one time, be prepared to provide detailed information as to why you stayed outside of the country for so long. If for education reasons – provide proof of attending school, for job reasons – bring a letter from your employer, because of illness – bring proof of your seeking medical attention.

It is up to the Immigration Officer to determine whether your permanent place of residence is in the United States, and there was good reason for you to have to remain outside of the country for > 6 months. Officers will look to the exact reasons for your staying longer outside the country.

In the past 5 years, you must have spent at least > ½ of that time in the United States. This means out of 1,825 days; you must have spent > 913 days in the United States. If you have not – you do not qualify for naturalization.

Did you ever serve in the military? When? What branch?

How you received permanent residency?

If you obtained permanent residency through a spouse – are you still married to that spouse? Bring proof with you including joint filed tax returns, bank account statements, insurance statements, proof of residency. If you are divorced – bring your divorce decree (issued by a court) and be ready to explain why you were divorced.

If you obtained permanent residency through an employer – be prepared to give information about your sponsoring employer, the name of the owner, address and telephone of the company, and the occupation you were sponsored in for permanent residency. The officer may also ask if you had experience in that occupation before being sponsored, and where you were working to gain that experience.

Your eligibility for citizenship – most asked questions – see later questions for a full listing.

Did you ever claim to be a US Citizen?

The immigration service has been adopting a strict approach to this question. If you have ever stated that you were a citizen, you can expect to be denied and the Immigration Service to start proceedings against you to lose your permanent residence.

Did you ever vote or register to vote in an American election?

Did you ever discriminate against anyone?

Did you ever lie to immigration/ use false documents?

Do you owe any taxes?

Did you ever file taxes as a nonresident (after receiving your permanent residency)?

Do you have a title of nobility?

Were you ever a member of the military?

If so – was it mandatory? When did you serve? What was your title/rank?

Do you have any weapons training?

If so – what kind of weapons?

Are you a member of a terrorist or socialist organization?

If a male, did you live in the US between ages 18-26? Did you register for Selective Service?

Be prepared to provide proof of the registration which you can obtain by checking the Selective Service Administration at https://www.sss.gov/Home/Verification

Citizenship Issues

Are you ready to take the oath of allegiance?

Did you read and understand the oath? (copy in this book)

If the law requires, are you ready to sign up to the military and defend the United States?

If the law requires, are you ready to assist the government in a civilian capacity in a time of national emergency?

OATH

You will be asked if you are ready to take the Oath of Citizenship. You should be familiar with what the oath says, but do not have to memorize it. The oath generally says that you will be loyal to the United States and defend this country.

I hereby declare, on oath, that I absolutely and entirely renounce and abjure all allegiance and fidelity to any foreign prince, potentate, state, or sovereignty, of whom or which I have heretofore been a subject or citizen; that I will support and defend the Constitution and laws of the

United States of America against all enemies, foreign and domestic; that I will bear true faith and allegiance to the same; that I will bear arms on behalf of the United States when required by the law; that I will perform noncombatant service in the Armed Forces of the United States when required by the law; that I will perform work of national importance under civilian direction when required by the law; and that I take this obligation freely, without any mental reservation or purpose of evasion; so help me God."

TEST

1. 10 Questions (6 correct)

2. Read a Question Out Loud

3. Write a Sentence

Three Tests for Citizenship

Most applicants for citizenship or naturalization as it is called, are subject to THREE different "tests" when applying. It is important that an individual understand that in applying for Citizenship their entire immigration history is being reviewed and an Immigration Officer is making a determination not only over whether an applicant passes a test, but moreover, is reviewing the applicant's entire immigration history.

The Citizenship process should be looked upon as a complex, detailed demanding process, not just the completion of a form and passing of a simple civics test. This is not a process that should be taken lightly.

Often persons get "free" help with benevolent charities completing applications during large scale meetings. However, an applicant can face severe consequences including the loss of their permanent residency and even removal from the United States if certain matters come to the attention of an Immigration Officer reviewing your application.

First and foremost are persons who have ever been arrested, detained, or even stopped by a Police Officer. These individuals should ensure they seek the assistance of an attorney to review their criminal record before proceeding with the filing of an application for Citizenship.

Each Applicant for Citizenship undergoes three tests:

1. Test of Civics/History/Government, Reading & Writing

a. Civics/history test of 10 questions chosen out of a possible 100

b. Reading – applicants will be asked to read out loud a

sample sentence from a fixed set of possible sentences

c. Writing – applicants will be asked to write a sentence

dictated by an Immigration Officer.

2. Ability to Communicate in English

a. The Immigration Officer will review your application with

you. Traditionally, this takes place after you pass your test.

This portion can be difficult for those that do not speak

English well.

b. The Immigration Officer will speak to you in English to

determine if you generally can communicate.

3. Eligibility –a review of an Applicant's personal history

a. The Immigration Officer will review your entire immigration

file and determine if you have the proper character to

become a citizen. The Officer will literally have before them

your entire immigration history including every form and

piece of paper that you submitted to the Immigration Service.

This includes your applications for immigration benefits

before permanent residency.

i. The Officer will review how you obtained your green card or permanent residency.

1. If you received your permanent residency through marriage to a US Citizen, then the Immigration Officer will ask questions about your marriage. The Officer can question whether the marriage was legitimate.

2. If you received your permanent residency through a family member – the Immigration Officer will review your original application to make sure there were no improprieties when you applied.

3. If you received your permanent residency through an employer – the Immigration Officer can ask you questions about the employer and the employment relationship.

ii. The Officer will review your criminal background – checking if you were ever arrested/detained/stopped by a Police Officer at home or abroad.

1. For the Immigration Service- to be stopped, arrested, or detained means precisely that – any time a Police agency would take your fingerprints

a. Regardless of the eventual outcome of the case – or what you think it means to be arrested – you will be expected to admit to all times that you were arrested/stopped or detained by a Police agency.

i. Sometimes applicants believe that an arrest means serving time in jail. But the Immigration Service has a much broader interpretation – including anytime that a Police agency would take your fingerprints and record the information.

ii. The Immigration Service obtains criminal background information on individuals primarily from the FBI. The FBI retains this information forever, regardless of expungements, or local agencies clearing of a criminal history.

AMERICAN GOVERNMENT
GOUVERNEMENT AMERICAIN

Principles of American Democracy
Principes de la Démocratie Américaine

1. What is the supreme law of the land?
The Constitution

1. Quelle est la loi suprème de la Patrie?
- La Constitution

2. What does the Constitution do?
Sets up the government
Defines the government
Protects basic rights of Americans

2. Qu'est-ce que fait la Constitution?
- Organizer le gouvernement
- Définir le gouvernement
- Protéger les droix fondamentaux des Americains

3. The idea of self-government is in the first three words of the Constitution. What are these words?
We the People

3. L'idée d'un gouvernement à sois-même est definit par les trois premiers mots de
la Constitution. Quels sont ces trois mots?
- Nous le Peuple

* If you are 65 years or older, and you are a permanent resident for 20 years or more, you can study just the questions that have an asterisk.

*Si vous avez 65 ans ou plus, et vous êtes un résident permanent pendant 20 ans ou plus,
vous pouvez étudier seulement les questions qui ont un astérisque.
Services de Citoyenneté et d'

4. What is an amendment?
A change to the Constitution.
An addition to the Constitution.

4. Qu'est-ce qu'est un amendement?
- Un changement (de la Constitution)
- Une addition (à la Constitution)
5. What do we call the first ten amendments to the Constitution?
The Bill of Rights

5. Qu'est-ce qu'on appelle les dix premiers amendements de la Constitution?
- La Déclaration des Droits de l'Homme

6. What is one right or freedom from the First Amendment? * (You need to know one answer)
Speech
Religion
Assembly
Press
Petition the government

6. Quel est un droit ou une liberté du premier amendement?*
- Parole
- Religion
- Assemblée
- Presse
- Présenter un pétition au gouvernement

7. How many amendments does the Constitution have?
Twenty-seven (27)

7. Combien d'amendements à la Constitution?
- Vingt-sept (27)

8. What did the Declaration of Independence do?
Announced our independence (from Great Britain)
Declared our independence (from Great Britain)
Said that the United States is free (from Great Britain)

8. Qu'est-ce qu'a fait la Déclaration d'Indépendence?

- Annoncer notre Indépendence (de la Grande Bretagne)
- Déclarer notre Indépendence (de la Grande Bretagne)
- Dire que les Etats-Unis est libre (de la Grande Bretagne)

9. What are two rights in the Declaration of Independence?
Life
Liberty
Pursuit of Happiness

9. Quels sont deux droits de la Déclaration d'Indépendence?
- La Vie
- La Liberté
- La Poursuite du Bonheur
10. What is freedom of religion?
You can practice any religion, or not practice a religion.

10.Qu'est-ce que c'est la liberté de religion?
- Vous pouvez pratiquer n'importe quelle religion ou ne pas pratiquer aucune
religion

11. What is the economic system in the United States?*
capitalist economy
market economy

11.Quel est le système économique des Etats-Unis?*
- Economie capitaliste
- Economie de marché

12. What is the "rule of law"?
Everyone must follow the law
Leaders must obey the law.
Government must obey the law.
No one is above the law

12.Quel est le "règlement de la loi" (rule of law)
- Tout le monde doit suivre la loi
- Les têtes de gouvernement doivent suivre la loi
- Le gouvernement doit suivre la loi
- Personne n'est au-dessus de la loi

System of Government

Le Système de Gouvernement

13. Name one branch or part of the government.*
Congress
Legislative
President
Executive
The courts
Judicial

13.Citez une branche du gouvernement *
- Congrès
- Législatif
- Président
- Executif
- Les tribunaux
- Judiciaire

14. What stops one branch of government from becoming too powerful?
Checks and balances
Separation of powers

14. Qu'est-ce qui arrete une branche du gouvernement d'avoir trop de pouvoir?
- Chèques et balances
- Séparation des pouvoirs

15. Who is in charge of the executive branch?
The President

15.Qui est en charge de la branche executive?
- Le Président

16. Who makes federal laws?
Congress
Senate and House of Representatives

U.S. legislature

16.Qui fait les lois fédérales?
- Le Congrès
- Le Sénat et la Chambre des Représentants
- La Legislature(des Etats-Unis ou nationale

17. What are the two parts of the U.S. Congress?*
The Senate and House of Representatives

17.Quelles sont les deux parts du Congrès des Etats-Unis?*
- Le Sénat et la Chambre des Représentants

18. How many U.S. Senators are there?
One hundred (100)

18.Il y a combien de sénateurs?
- Cent (100)

19. We elect a U.S. Senator for how many years?
Six (6)

19.Nous élisons un Senateur des Etats-Unis pour combien
d'années?
- Six (6)

20. Who is one of your state's U.S. Senators?*
See list below. Answers will vary. For District of Columbia
residents and residents of U.S. territories, the answer is that D.C.
(or the territory where the applicant lives) has no U.S. Senators.
20.Qui est un de vos sénateurs des Etats-Unis maintenant?*

- La réponse peut varier. [Les résidents du District de Colombia et
les résidents
des territoires des Etats-Unis doivent répondre que DC (ou le
territoire où ils
vivent) n'a pas de sénateur .

See the back of the book and write your answer here:

____

* If you are 65 years old or older and have been a legal permanent resident of the United States for 20 or more years, you may study just the questions that have been marked with an asterisk.

*Si vous avez 65 ans ou plus, et vous êtes un résident permanent pendant 20 ans ou plus,
vous pouvez étudier seulement les questions qui ont un astérisque. 23.Dites le nom de votre Représentant des Etats-Unis
21. The House of Representatives has how many voting members?
Four hundred thirty-five (435)

21.La Chambre des Représentants a combien de membres qui votent?
- Quatre-cent trente-cinq (435)
22. We elect a U.S. Representative for how many years?
Two (2)

22. Nous élisons un Représentant des Etats-Unis pour combien d'années?
- Deux (2)

23. Name your U.S. Representative.
Answers will vary. [Residents of territories with nonvoting Delegates or resident Commissioners may provide the name of that Delegate or Commissioner. Also acceptable is any statement that the territory has no (voting) Representatives in Congress.]

23.Dites le nom de votre Représentant des Etats-Unis
- La réponse peut varier les résidents des territoires avec des délégats qui ne
votent pas ou des commissaires résidents peuvent donner le nom de ce
délégat ou du commissaire. Aussi, un énoncé qui dise que le territoire n'a pas
de représentant au congrès qui puisse voter est acceptable.

Members of the 114th Congress

You must determine what district you live in to identify your Representative.

Usted debe determiner qué distrito vive en identificar a su representante

Representatives are subject to change./ Los representantes están sujetos a cambios

See the back of the book and write your answer here:

---

24. Who does a U.S. Senator represent?
All people of the state

24.Un sénateur des Etats-Unis représente qui?
- Tout le peuple de cet Etat

25. Why do some states have more Representatives than other states?
There are three correct answers. You need to know one answer.
Because of the state's population
Because they have more people
Because some states have more people
25.Pourquoi il y a des Etats qui ont plus de représentants que d'autres?
- à cause de la population de cet Etat
- parcequ'ils ont plus de gens
- parceque certains Etats ont plus de gens

26. We elect a President for how many years?
Four (4)

26.Nous élisons un Président pour combien d'années?
- Quatre (4)

27. In what month do we vote for President?*
November

27.Pendant quel mois nous avons les élections?*
- Novembre

28. What is the name of the President of the United States now?*
Joe Biden

28.Quel est le nom du Président des Etats-Unis maintenant?*
- Joe Biden

29. What is the name of the Vice President of the United States now?
Kamala Harris.

29.Quel est le nom du Vice-Président des Etats-Unis maintenant?
Kamala Harris
30. If the President can no longer serve, who becomes President?
The Vice President

30.Si le Président ne peut plus servir, qui devient le Président?
- Le Vice-President

31. If both the President and the Vice President can no longer serve, who becomes President?
The Speaker of the House

31. Si le Vice-Président ne peut pas servir, qui devient le Président?
- Le Président (speaker) de la Chambre

32. Who is the Commander in Chief of the military?
The President

32.Qui est le Commendant en Chef de l'armée?
- Le Président

33. Who signs bills to become laws?
The President

33.Qui signe les projets de loi pour devenir des lois?
- Le Président

34. Who vetoes bills?
The President

34.Qui met son veto à un projet de loi?
- Le Président

35. What does the President's Cabinet do?
Advises the President

35.Que fait le cabinet du Président?
- Conseiller le Président

36. What are two Cabinet-level positions?
Secretary of State
Secretary of Labor

36.Quels sont deux positions à niveau de cabinet?
- Ministre de l'Agriculture
- Ministre du Commerce
- Ministre de la Défense
- Ministre d'Education
- Ministre de l'Energie
- Ministre de la Santé et de Services Humains
- Ministre de la Securité de la Patrie
- Ministre du Logement et d'Urbanization
- Ministre Intérieur
- Ministre du Travail
- Ministre de l'Etat
- Ministre du Transport
- Ministre de Trésorerie
- Ministre d'Affaires des Vétérans
- Ministre de la Justice
- Vice-Président

37. What does the judicial branch do?
Reviews laws
Explains laws
Resolves disputes (disagreements)

decides if a law goes against the Constitution

37.Que fait la Branche Judiciaire?
- Réviser les lois
- Expliquer les lois
- Résoudre des disputes (désaccords)
- Decider si une loi est contre la Constitution

38. What is the highest court in the United States?
The Supreme Court

38.Quelle est le tribunal le plus haut des Etats-Unis?
- La Cour Suprême

39. How many justices are on the Supreme Court?
Nine (9)

39.Combien de juges sont dans la Cour Suprême?
- Neuf (9)
40. Who is the Chief Justice of the United States?
John G. Roberts, Jr.

40.Qui est le Chef de Justice des Etats-Unis maintenant?
- John Roberts (John G. Roberts, Jr.)

41. Under our Constitution, some powers belong to the federal
government. What is one power of the federal government?
Know one of the following:
To print money
To declare war
To create an army
To make treaties

41.Selon nôtre Constitution, certains pouvoirs appartiennent au
Gouvernement
Fédéral. Citez un pouvoir du Gouvernement Fédéral.
- Imprimer de l'argent
- Déclarer la guerre
- Créer une armée
- Faire des traités

42. Under our Constitution, some powers belong to the states.
What is one power of the states?
Provide schooling and education

42.Selon nôtre Constitution, certains pouvoirs appartiennent au Gouvernement de
chaque Etat. Citez un pouvoir de l'Etat.
- Pourvoir de l'Instruction et de l'éducation
- Pourvoir de la protection (police)
- Pourvoir de la sécurité (pompiers)
- Donner des permis de conduire
- Approuver la réglementation urbaine et l'utilization de la terre

43. Who is the Governor of your state?
Answers will vary. Residents of the District of Columbia and U.S. territories without a Governor should say "we don't have a Governor."

43.Qui est le Gouverneur de votre Etat maintenant?
- La réponse peut varier. (les résidents du District de Columbia doivent
répondre que D.C n'a pas de gouverneur)
State Governors
Governors are subject to change.
Source:
http://en.wikipedia.org/wiki/List_of_current_United_States_govern ors_January 2018

See the back of the book and write your answer here:

____

44. What is the capital of your state?*
Answers will vary. District of Columbia residents should answer that D.C. is not a state and does not have a capital. Residents of U.S. territories should name the capital of the territory.

44.Quelle est la capitale de votre Etat?*
- La réponse peut varier. (les résidents du District de Columbia doivent
répondre que D.C. n'est pas un Etat et n'a pas de capitale. Les résidents
des térritoires des Etats-Unis doivent donner le nom de la capitale de leur
térritoire).¿Cual es la capital de tu estado? *
Las respuestas variarán. Los residentes del distrito de Columbia
deben contestar a que la D.C. no es un estado y no tienen una
capital. Los residentes de los territorios de los E.E.U.U. deben
nombrar la capital del territorio.

See the back of the book and write your answer here:

____

45. What are the two major political parties in the United States?*
Democratic and Republican

45.Quels sont les deux partis politiques les plus importants aux
Etats-Unis?*
- Démocrat et Républicain

46. What is the political party of the President now?
Republ;ican Party

46.Quel est le parti politique du Président maintenant?
- Parti Démocrat

47. What is the name of the Speaker of the House of
Representatives now?
Kevin McCarthy

47.Quel est le nom du Speaker de la Chambre de
Représentatives?
- Kevin McCarthy

C: Rights and Responsibilities
C: Droits et Responsabilités

48. There are four amendments to the Constitution about who can vote. Describe one of them.
Citizens eighteen (18) and older can vote.
Any citizen can vote. (Women and men can vote.)

48.Il y a quatre amendements à la Constitution sur qui a le droit de voter. Décrivez
un de ces droits.
- Les citoyens qui ont 18 ans ou plus peuvent voter.
- Vous ne devez pas payer un impot pour voter
- Touts les citoyens peuvent voter (femmes et hommes)
- Un homme citoyen de n'importe quelle race peut voter

49. What is one responsibility that is only for United States citizens?*
Serve on a jury

49.Quelle est une responsabilité seulement pour les citoyens des Etats-Unis?*
- Servir dans un jury
- Voter dans une election fédérale

50. What are two rights only for United States citizens?
Apply for a federal job
vote

50.Citez un droit que seulement les citoyens des Etats-Unis ont.
- Voter dans une election fédérale
- Se presenter pour les elections fédérales

51. What are two rights of everyone living in the United States?
Freedom of expression
Freedom of speech
51.Quels sont deux droits de toutes les personnes qui vivent aux Etats-Unis?
- Liberté d'expression
- Liberté de parole
- Liberté de réunion

- Liberté de présenter une pétition au Gouvernement
-

52. What do we show loyalty to when we say the Pledge of Allegiance?
The United States and the flag

52.Quand nous disons le Pledge of Allegiance (la Promesse d'allégeance), à quoi
montrons-nous loyauté?
- Aux Etats-Unis
- Au drapeau
53. What is one promise you make when you become a United States citizen?
Defend the Constitution and laws of the United States

53.Quelle est une promesse que vous faites quand vous devennez un citoyen des
Etats-Unis?
- Abandonner la loyauté à d'autres pays
- Défendre la Constitution et les lois des Etats-Unis
- Obéir aux lois des Etats-Unis
- Servir dans l'armée des Etats-Unis (si nécéssaire)
- Servir la Nation (avec du travail important, si nécéssaire)
- Etre loyal aux Etats-Unis

54. How old do citizens have to be to vote?*
Eighteen (18) and older

54.A quel age peut un citoyen des Etats-Unis voter?*
- Dix-huit (18) et plus

55. What are two ways that Americans can participate in their democracy?
Vote
Join a political party

55.Quelles sont deux façons par lesquelles un citoyen des Etats-Unis peut participer
dans sa démocratie?
- Voter

- Joindre un parti politique
- Aider pendant une campagne
- Joindre un groupe civic
- Joindre un groupe de la communauté
- Donner votre opinion sur un point à un officiel élu
- Appeler des Senateurs et des Représentatifs
- Appuyer ou s'opposer publiquement à un point ou à une loi
- Poser sa candidature pour une position
- Ecrire à un journal

56. When is the last day you can send in federal income tax forms?*
April 15

56.Quel est le dernier jour que vous pouvez envoyez la déclaration de revenues?*
- 15 d'avril

57. When must all men register for the Selective Service?
Between eighteen (18) and twenty-six (26)

57.Quand est-ce que touts les hommes doivent s' enregistrer pour le Service Selectif?
- Dix-huit ans (18)
- De dix-huit (18) à vingt-six (26) ans

AMERICAN HISTORY

HISTOIRE AMÉRICAINE

Colonial Period and Independence
Période Coloniale et Indépendence

58. What is one reason colonists came to America?
Freedom
Political liberty

58.Donnez une raison pour laquelle les colons sont venus en
Amérique.
- Liberté
- Liberté politique
- Liberté de religion
- Opportunité économique
- Pour pratiquer leur religion
- Echapper la persécution

59. Who lived in America before the Europeans arrived?
Native Americans
American Indians

59.Qui vivait en Amérique avant que les Européens arrivent?
- Les Indiens Américains
- Les Américains natifs

60. What group of people was taken to America and sold as
slaves?
Africans

60.Quel groupe de personnes furent apportée en Amerique et
vendue comme
esclaves?
- Africains
- Des gens d'Afrique

61. Why did the colonists fight the British?
Because of high taxes (taxation without representation)
Because the British army stayed in their houses (boarding,
quartering)
Because they didn't have self-government
61.Pourquoi les colons se sont combattu avec les Anglais?
- A cause des impots très hauts (impots sans représentation)
- Parceque l'armée anglaise restait dans leurs maisons (pension
et
logement)

62. Who wrote the Declaration of Independence?
Thomas Jefferson

62.Qui a écrit la Déclaration d'Indépendence?
- (Thomas) Jefferson

63. When was the Declaration of Independence adopted?
July 4, 1776

63.Quand est-ce que la Déclaration d'Indépendence a été
adoptée?
- 4 Juillet, 1776

64. There were 13 original states. Name three.
New York
New Jersey
Virgina

64.Il y avait 13 Etats au début. Donnez le nom de trois.
- New Hampshire
- Massachusets
- Rhode Island
- Connecticut
- New York
- New Jersey
- Pennsylvannia
- Delaware
- Maryland
- Virginia
- North Carolina

- South Carolina
- Georgia

65. What happened at the Constitutional Convention?
The Constitution was written.

65.Qu'est-ce qui c'est passé pendant l'Assemblée
Constitutionnelle?
- On a écrit la Constitution
- Les Pères Fondateurs de la Nation ont écrit la Constitution

66. When was the Constitution written?
1787

66.Quand est-ce que la Constitution a été écrite?
- 1787

67. The Federalist Papers supported the passage of the U.S.
Constitution. Name one of the writers.
James Madison

67.Les Documents Fédéralistes ont appuyer le passage de la
Constitution. Citez un
des écrivains.
- (James) Madison
- (Alexander) Hamilton
- (John) Jay

68. What is one thing Benjamin Franklin is famous for?
U.S. diplomat

68.Citez une chose pour laquelle Benjamin Franklin est célèbre.
- Diplomate des Etats-Unis
- Le membre le plus vieux de l'Assemblée Constitutionnelle
- Premier Administrateur Général des Etats-Unis
- Ecrivain de "Poor Richard's Almanac" (Almanach du Pauvre
Richard)
- Fondateur des premieres bibliothèques

69.Qui est le "Père de notre Patrie"?
- (George) Washington

69. Who is the "Father of Our Country"?
George Washington

69.Qui est le "Père de notre Patrie"?
- (George) Washington

70. Who was the first President?*
George Washington

70.Qui est le premier Président?*
- (George Washington)

71. What territory did the United States buy from France in 1803?
The Louisiana Territory

71.Quel territoire ont acheté les Etats-Unis de la France en 1803?
- Le térritoire de la Louisiane
- La Louisiane

72. Name one war fought by the United States in the 1800s.
Spanish-American War
72.Donnez le nom d'une guerre que les Etats-Unis ont combatuent de 1800 à 1900.
- La guerre de 1812
- La guerre des Etats-Unis contre le Mexique
- La guerre civile
- La guerre des Etats-Unis contre l'Espagne

73. Name the U.S. war between the North and the South.
The Civil War

73.Donnez le nom de la guerre des Etats-Unis entre le Nord et le Sud.
- La guerre civile
- La guerre entre les Etats

74. Name one problem that led to the Civil War.
Slavery

74.Donnez le nom d'un problème qui fut une raison pour la guerre civile.
- L'esclavage
- Des raisons économiques
- Les droits des Etats

75. What was one important thing that Abraham Lincoln did?*
Freed the slaves (Emancipation Proclamation)

75.Citez une chose importante que Abraham Lincoln fit. *
- Libérer les esclaves (Proclamation d'Emancipation)
- Sauver (ou préserver) l'Union
- Conduire les Etats-Unis pendant la guerre civile
76. What did the Emancipation Proclamation do?
Freed the slaves

76.Que fit la Proclamation d'Emancipation?
- Libérer les esclaves
- Libérer les esclaves dans la Confédération
- Libérer les esclaves dans les Etats Confedérés
- Libérer les esclaves dans la plus part des Etats du Sud

77. What did Susan B. Anthony do?
Fought for women's rights

77.Qu'est-ce Susan B. Anthony fit?
- Défendre les droits des femmes
- Defendre les droits de l'homme

C: Recent American History and Other Important Historical Information

C: Histoire récente des Etats-Unis et d'autre information historique importante

78. Name one war fought by the United States in the 1900s.*
World War II

78.Citez une guerre combatue par les Etats-Unis pendant le vingtième siècle.*
- La première Guerre Mondiale
- La deuxième Guerre Mondiale
- La guerre de Corée
- La guerre du Vietnam
- La guerre du Golfe (Persique)

79. Who was President during World War I?
Woodrow Wilson

79.Qui était le Président pendant la Première Guerre Mondiale?
- (Woodrow) Wilson

80. Who was President during the Great Depression and World War II?
Franklin Roosevelt

80.Qui était le Président pendant la Grande Dépréssion et le deuxième Guerre
Mondiale?
- (Franklin) Roosevelt

81. Who did the United States fight in World War II?
Japan, Germany and Italy

81.Les Etats-Unis ont combattu quels pays pendant la deuxième Guerre Mondiale?
- Le Japon, l'Alemagne et l'Italie

82. Before he was President, Eisenhower was a general. What war was he in?
World War II

82.Avant d'être le Président, Eisenhower était un général. Dans quelle guerre était-il?
- Deuxième Guerre Mondiale

83. During the Cold War, what was the main concern of the United States?
Communism

83.Pendant la Guerre Froide, quel était le problème le plus important pour les EtatsUnis?
- Le Communisme
84. What movement tried to end racial discrimination?
civil rights movement

84.Quel mouvement a essayé de terminer la discrimination raciale?
- Le mouvement des droits civiques

85. What did Martin Luther King, Jr. do?*
Fought for civil rights

85.Qu'est-ce que Martin Luther King, Jr fit?*
- Défendre les droits civiques
- Travailler pour l'égalité de touts les Américains

86. What major event happened on September 11, 2001 in the United States?
Terrorists attacked the United States.

86.Quel événement très important c'est passé le 11 de Septembre, 2001
- L'attaque par des térroristes sur les Etats-Unis

87. Name one American Indian tribe in the United States.
Cherokee
Navajo
Apache

 [Adjudicators will be supplied with a complete list.] [Suministrarán una lista completa.]

87.Citez une tribu indienne americaine dans les Etats-Unis. (les officiers du USCIS
auront une liste de tribus indiennes americaines reconnues fédéralement)

- Cherokee
- Navajo
- Sioux
- Chippewa
- Choctaw
- Pueblo
- Apache
- Iroquois
- Creek
- Blackfeet
- Seminole
- Cheyenne
- Arawak
- Shawnee
- Mohegan
- Huron

INTEGRATED CIVICS

ETUDES CIVIQUES INTEGREES

Geography / Geographie

88. Name one of the two longest rivers in the United States.
Missouri or Mississippi river

88.Citez un des deux fleuves les plus longs des Etats-Unis
- Missouri
- Mississippi

89. What ocean is on the West Coast of the United States?
Pacific Ocean

89.Quel océan est sur la côte de l' Ouest des Etats-Unis?
- L'océan Pacifique

90. What ocean is on the East Coast of the United States?
Atlantic Ocean

90. Quel océan est sur la côte de l'Est des Etats-Unis?
- L'océan Atlantique

91. Name one U.S. territory.
Puerto Rico

91.Citez un territoire des Etats-Unis.
- Puerto Rico
- U.S. Virgin Islands
- Samoa Américaine
- Iles Mariana du Nord
- Guam

92. Name one state that borders Canada.
New York

92.Citez un Etat qui fait frontière avec le Canada
- Maine
- New Hampshire
- Vermont
- New York
- Pennsylvania
- Ohio
- Michigan
- Minnesota
- North Dakota

93. Name one state that borders Mexico.
California

93.Citez un Etat qui fait frontière avec le Mexique
- California
- Arizona
- New Mexico
- Texas

94. What is the capital of the United States?*
Washington, D.C.

94.Quelle est la capitale des Etats-Unis?*
- Washington, D.C.

95. Where is the Statue of Liberty?*
New York Harbor
Other acceptable answers are: New Jersey, near the city of New York, and
the Hudson River

95.Où est la Statue de la Liberté?*
- New York (Le port)
D'autres réponses acceptables sont: New Jersey, près de la cité de New York, et sur
le fleuve Hudson

Symbols / Signes

96. Why does the flag have 13 stripes?
Because there were 13 original colonies

96.Pourquoi le drapeau a 13 bandes?
- Parcequ'il y avait 13 colonies originales
- Parceque les bandes representent les colonies originales

97. Why does the flag have 50 stars?*
Because there is one star for each state

97.Pourquoi le drapeau a 50 étoiles?*
- Parcequ'il y a une étoile pour chaque Etat
- Parceque chaque étoile représente un Etat
- Parcequ'il y a 50 Etats

98. What is the name of the national anthem?
The Star-Spangled Banner

98.Quel est le nom de l'hymne national?
- Le Star-Spangle Banner

Holidays. / Jours fériés

99. When do we celebrate Independence Day?*
July 4

99.Quand est-ce que nous célébrons le Jour de l'Indépendence?*
- 4 Juillet

100. Name two national U.S. holidays.
Independence Day
Christmas

100. Citez deux jours nationaux fériés des Etats-Unis.
- Le nouvel an
- Le jour de Martin Luther King, Jr.
- Le jour des Présidents

SAMPLE WRITTEN SENTENCES

You will be asked to write a sample sentence. Normally you can make up to three (3) errors in writing and still pass the test.

Be careful to listen to each word the examiner reads. Make sure to write each word, even if you think it is not needed grammatically, if the examiner reads a word; please write out every word that is dictated.

1) A senator is elected for 6 years.

2) Kamala Harris is the Vice President of the United States.

3) All people want to be free.

4) America is the land of freedom.

5) All American citizens have the right to vote.

6) America is the home of the brave.

7) America is the land of the free.

8) Joe Biden is the President of the United States.

9) Citizens have the right to vote.

10) Congress is part of the American government.

11) Congress meets in Washington DC.

12) Congress passes laws in the United States.

13) George Washington was the first president.

14) I want to be a citizen of the United States.

15) I want to be an American citizen.

16) I want to become an American so I can vote.

17) It is important for all citizens to vote.

18) Many people come to America for freedom.

19) Many people have died for freedom.

20) Martha Washington was the first lady.

21) Only Congress can declare war.

22) Our Government is divided into three branches.

23) People in America have the right to freedom.

24) People vote for the President in November.

25) The American flag has stars and stripes.

26) The American flag has 13 stripes.

27) The capital of the United States is Washington DC.

28) The colors of the flag are red white and blue.

29) The Constitution is the supreme law of our land.

30) The flag of the United States has 50 stars.

31) The House and Senate are parts of Congress

32) The President enforces the laws.

33) The President has the power of veto.

34) The President is elected every 4 years.

35) The President lives in the White House.

36) The President lives in Washington D.C.

37) The President must be an American citizen.

38) The President must be born in the United States.

39) The President signs bills into law.

40) The stars of the American flag are white.

41) The White House is in Washington, DC.

42) The United States flag is red white and blue.

43) The United States of America has 50 states.

Members of the Senate

Representatives are subject to change.

Find your state to identify your two Senators

Source: http://Senate.gov Updated January 2018

What is a class? - Article I, section 3 of the Constitution requires the Senate to be divided into three classes for purposes of elections. Senators are elected to six-year terms, and every two years the members of one class—approximately one-third of the senators—face election or reelection. Terms for senators in Class I expire in 2019, Class II in 2021, and Class III in 2023.

U.S. State Postal Abbreviations List

Alabama – AL   Alaska – AK   Arizona – AZ   Arkansas - AR

California – CA   Colorado – CO   Connecticut - CT

Delaware – DE   District of Columbia - DC

Florida - FL

Georgia - GA

Hawaii - HI

Idaho – ID   Illinois – IL   Indiana – IN   Iowa - IA

Kansas – KS   Kentucky - KY

Louisiana - LA

Maine – ME   Maryland – MD   Massachusetts – MA
Michigan – MI   Minnesota – MN   Mississippi – MS
Missouri – MO   Montana - MT

Nebraska – NE   Nevada – NV   New Hampshire – NH
New Jersey – NJ   New Mexico – NM   New York – NY
North Carolina – NC   North Dakota - ND

Ohio – OH   Oklahoma – OK   Oregon - OR

Pennsylvania - PA

Rhode Island - RI

South Carolina – SC   South Dakota - SD

Tennessee – TN   Texas - TX

Utah - UT

Vermont – VT   Virginia - VA

Washington – WA   West Virginia – WV   Wisconsin – WI
Wyoming - WY

US Commonwealth and Territories

American Samoa – AS   Federated States of Micronesia – FM
Guam – GU   Marshall Islands - MH

Northern Mariana Islands – MP   Palau – PW   Puerto Rico –
PR   Virgin Islands

Senators of the 118th Congress

Class - Article I, section 3 of the Constitution requires the Senate
to be divided into three classes for purposes of elections.
Senators are elected to six-year terms, and every two years the
members of one class—approximately one-third of the senators—
face election or reelection.

Tommy Tuberville   Republican   Alabama

Katie Britt   Republican   Alabama

Lisa Murkowski   Republican   Alaska

Dan Sullivan Republican   Alaska

Kyrsten Sinema   Democratic   Arizona

Mark Kelly   Democratic   Arizona

John Boozman   Republican   Arkansas

Tom Cotton   Republican   Arkansas

Dianne Feinstein Democratic   California

Alex Padilla   Democratic   California

Michael Bennet   Democratic   Colorado

John Hickenlooper   Democratic   Colorado

Richard Blumenthal   Democratic   Connecticut

Chris Murphy   Democratic   Connecticut

Tom Carper Democratic Delaware

Chris Coons Democratic Delaware

Marco Rubio Republican Florida

Rick Scott Republican Florida

Jon Ossoff Democratic Georgia

Brian Schatz Democratic Hawaii

Mazie Hirono Democratic Hawaii

Mike Crapo Republican Idaho

Jim Risch Republican Idaho

Dick Durbin Democratic Illinois

Tammy Duckworth Democratic Illinois

Todd Young Republican Indiana

Mike Braun Republican Indiana

Chuck Grassley Republican Iowa

Joni Ernst Republican Iowa

Jerry Moran Republican Kansas

Roger Marshall Republican Kansas

Mitch McConnell Republican Kentucky

Rand Paul Republican Kentucky

Bill Cassidy Republican Louisiana

John Neely Kennedy Republican Louisiana

Susan Collins Republican Maine

Angus King Independent Maine

Ben Cardin Democratic Maryland

Chris Van Hollen Democratic   Maryland

Elizabeth Warren Democratic   Massachusetts

Ed Markey   Democratic   Massachusetts

Debbie Stabenow   Democratic   Michigan

Gary Peters Democratic   Michigan

Amy Klobuchar   Democratic   Minnesota

Tina Smith   Democratic   Minnesota

Roger Wicker   Republican   Mississippi

Cindy Hyde-Smith   Republican   Mississippi

Josh Hawley Republican   Missouri

Eric Schmitt Republican   Missouri

Jon Tester   Democratic   Montana

Steve Daines   Republican   Montana

Deb Fischer Republican   Nebraska

Ben Sasse   Republican   Nebraska

TBD   Republican   Nebraska

Catherine Cortez Masto   Democratic   Nevada

Jacky Rosen Democratic   Nevada

Jeanne Shaheen Democratic   New Hampshire

Maggie Hassan   Democratic   New Hampshire

Bob Menendez   Democratic   New Jersey

Cory Booker Democratic   New Jersey

Martin Heinrich   Democratic   New Mexico

Ben Ray Luján   Democratic   New Mexico

Chuck Schumer   Democratic   New York

Kirsten Gillibrand Democratic   New York

Thom Tillis   Republican   North Carolina

Ted Budd   Republican   North Carolina

John Hoeven   Republican   North Dakota

Kevin Cramer   Republican   North Dakota

Sherrod Brown   Democratic   Ohio

J. D. Vance   Republican   Ohio

James Lankford   Republican   Oklahoma

Markwayne Mullin   Republican   Oklahoma

Ron Wyden   Democratic   Oregon

Jeff Merkley Democratic   Oregon

Bob Casey, Jr.   Democratic   Pennsylvania

John Fetterman   Democratic   Pennsylvania

Jack Reed   Democratic   Rhode Island

Sheldon Whitehouse Democratic   Rhode Island

Lindsey Graham Republican   South Carolina

Tim Scott   Republican   South Carolina

John Thune   Republican   South Dakota

Mike Rounds Republican   South Dakota

Marsha Blackburn   Republican   Tennessee

Bill Hagerty   Republican   Tennessee

John Cornyn Republican   Texas

Ted Cruz   Republican   Texas

Mike Lee   Republican   Utah

Mitt Romney Republican   Utah

Bernie Sanders   Independent Vermont

Peter Welch *   Democratic   Vermont

Mark Warner Democratic   Virginia

Tim Kaine   Democratic   Virginia

Patty Murray Democratic   Washington

Maria Cantwell   Democratic   Washington

Joe Manchin Democratic   West Virginia

Shelley Moore Capito Republican   West Virginia

Ron Johnson   Republican   Wisconsin

Tammy Baldwin Democratic   Wisconsin

John Barrasso   Republican   Wyoming

Cynthia Lummis Republican   Wyoming

List of State Governors

Governors are subject to change. District of Columbia residents should answer that D.C. is not a state and does not have a capital. Residents of U.S. territories should name the capital of the territory.

Source: http://en.wikipedia.org/wiki/List_of_current_United_States_governors
Governors are subject to change. District of Columbia residents should answer that D.C. is not a state and does not have a capital. Residents of U.S. territories should name the capital of the territory.

Source: https://en.wikipedia.org/wiki/List_of_current_United_States_gover nors

*Denotes newly elected Governors

Alabama – Kay Ivey

Alaska – Mike Dunaway

Arizona – To be determined

Arkansas – Asa Hutchinson.

California – Gavin Newsom

Colorado – Jared Polis

Connecticut – Ned Lamont

Delaware – John Carney

Florida – Ron DeSantis

Georgia – Brian Kemp

Hawaii – David Ige

Idaho – Brad Little

Illinois – J.B. Pritzker

Indiana – Eric Holcomb

Iowa – Kim Reynolds

Kansas – Laura Kelly

Kentucky – Andy Beshear

Louisiana – John Bel Edwards

Maine – Janet Mills

Maryland – Larry Hogan

Massachusetts – Charlie Baker

Michigan – Gretchen Whitmer

Minnesota – Tim Walz

Mississippi – Tate Reeves

Missouri – Mike Parson

Montana – Greg Gianforte*

Nebraska – Jim Pillen

Nevada – Steve Sisolak

New Hampshire – Chris Sununu

New Jersey – Phil Murphy

New Mexico – Michelle Lujan Grisham

New York – Kathy Hochul

North Carolina – Ray Cooper

North Dakota – Doug Burgum

Ohio – Mike DeWine

Oklahoma – Kevin Stitt

Oregon – Tina Kotek

Pennsylvania – Josh Shapiro

Rhode Island – Daniel McKee

South Carolina – Henri McMaster

South Dakota – Kristi Noem

Tennessee – Bill Lee

Texas – Greg Abbott

Utah – Spencer Cox

Vermont – Phil Scott

Virginia – Glenn Youngkin

Washington – Jay Inslee

West Virginia – Jim Justice

Wisconsin – Tony Evers

Wyoming – Mark Gordon

List of State Capitols

Alabama - Montgomery

Alaska - Juneau

Arizona - Phoenix

Arkansas - Little Rock

California - Sacramento

Colorado - Denver

Connecticut - Hartford

Delaware - Dover

Florida - Tallahassee

Georgia - Atlanta

Hawaii - Honolulu

Idaho - Boise

Illinois - Springfield

Indiana - Indianapolis

Iowa - Des Moines

Kansas - Topeka

Kentucky - Frankfort

Louisiana - Baton Rouge

Maine - Augusta

Maryland - Annapolis

Massachusetts - Boston

Michigan - Lansing

Minnesota - St. Paul

Mississippi - Jackson

Missouri - Jefferson City

Montana - Helena

Nebraska - Lincoln

Nevada - Carson City

New Hampshire - Concord

New Jersey - Trenton

New Mexico - Santa Fe

New York - Albany

North Carolina - Raleigh

North Dakota - Bismarck

Ohio - Columbus

Oklahoma - Oklahoma City

Oregon - Salem

Pennsylvania - Harrisburg

Rhode Island - Providence

South Carolina - Columbia

South Dakota - Pierre

Tennessee - Nashville

Texas - Austin

Utah - Salt Lake City

Vermont - Montpelier

Virginia - Richmond

Washington - Olympia

West Virginia - Charleston

Wisconsin - Madison

Wyoming – Cheyenne

ABOUT THE AUTHOR

Mike Swedenberg saw a need to assemble a study guide to help those persons wishing to immigrate to the United States whose second language is English. This study guide is annotated with the names of current Representatives that all applicants must know. The list is current for State Governors, US Senators and US Congressmen. This list will be updated at each election cycle.

Other books by the Author

A New York Wedding – a novel

Bully Boss – a novel

The Road Warrior a sales manual

Advertising Copywriting and the Unique Selling Proposition

Smart Money Stupid Money

21 ½ Things to Know Before Self-Publishing

How to Publish an eBook

How to Publish a Book in Print

The Short Stories by Mike Swedenberg